GW00728923

ART EYES

teaching and learning about visual arts in the primary classroom

• painting • sgraffito
• collage • drawing •

BOOK B

Published by User Friendly Resource Enterprises Ltd. Book No. 314B

Reihana MacDonald Robinson

Series Name: Art Eyes

Book Name: Book B: painting, sgraffito, collage, drawing
Book Number: 314 B
ISBN Number: ISBN: 1-877282-87-1
Published: June 2002

AUTHOR: Reihana MacDonald Robinson

ACKNOWLEDGEMENTS

The publisher wishes to acknowledge the work of the following people in the various stages of publishing this resource.

Design and Illustration: Akira Le Fevre

Editor: Pauline Scanlan

PUBLISHERS

User Friendly Resources Enterprises Ltd

New Zealand Office
PO Box 1820
Christchurch
Tel: 0508-500-393
Fax: 0508-500-399

Australian Office
PO Box 278
Annandale, NSW 2038
Tel: 1800-553-890
Fax: 1800-553-891

Distributed in Ireland by:
**Outside The Box
Learning Resources Ltd.**
Jigginstown Commercial Centre
Newbridge Road, Naas, County Kildare
Tel: 045 856344; Fax: 045 897819
Email: info@outsidetheboxlearning.com
www.otb.ie

WEBSITE:

Visit our on-line shop: www.userfr.com

COPYING NOTICE

COPYRIGHT

CONTENTS

ACKNOWLEDGEMENTS

The author wishes to thank all students and teachers and advisory colleagues from throughout the world who have helped inspire these texts. Their creative energies and spirited life forces have contributed to the manifestation of these books. A particular thanks is due to those children whose art work is shown in this book.

I would like to express my thanks to the children and teachers with whom I have had the pleasure of creating art. Thanks especially to children of Aotearoa/New Zealand, Pitcairn Island (first named Tama-ki-te-Rangi), Moorea andTahiti/French Polynesia, Kanaky/New Caledonia, Australia, France, San Juan and Santa Clara Pueblos of New Mexico, USA.

The invaluable mentoring kindly provided by Geoffrey Robinson is gratefully acknowledged. Thank you Noa Noa von Bassewitz for ongoing inspiration.

Many thanks to Akira Le Fevre, for the creative artwork and Pauline Scanlan at User Friendly Resources for her support and enthusiasm.

Nga mihi ki a koutou

INTRODUCTION

Art Eyes offers an approach to teaching visual arts that emphasises trusting what is seen and imagined. It is about giving courage to hearts so that art hands are free and confident to create visual images.

Art Eyes Book B presents an approach to teaching visual art based on the aims of contemporary visual arts education and art education research in Aotearoa/New Zealand, Australia and Scotland. This programme is designed sequentially within the parameters of the following four strands: Developing Practical Knowledge in the Visual Arts, Developing Ideas in the Visual Arts, Communicating and Interpreting in the Visual Arts and Understanding the Visual Arts in Context. It will identify the skills, knowledge and understandings that students can be expected to develop at these levels.

DEVELOPING PRACTICAL KNOWLEDGE IN THE VISUAL ARTS
This hands-on dimension of visual arts requires teachers to motivate students in the making of images and objects. Students will learn the elements of the art process, such as line, shape and texture. Through the use and knowledge of tools, technologies and materials they will create both two-dimensional and three-dimensional artworks in a variety of media.

DEVELOPING IDEAS IN THE VISUAL ARTS
Students will explore ideas through observation, imagination and inventive use of materials. At this level students are encouraged to use their own ideas and feelings, experiences and beliefs to use media expressively.

COMMUNICATING AND INTERPRETING IN THE VISUAL ARTS
Students learn to critically analyse and interpret their own and others' artwork. At this level students can compare and contrast design elements, use of
materials and subject matter. They use a growing art vocabulary (Art Words) and processes of creative thinking to describe how objects and images can communicate stories.

UNDERSTANDING THE VISUAL ARTS IN CONTEXT
Students will investigate the purpose and context of visual arts in past and present societies. They will learn to communicate ideas, feelings, experiences and beliefs that are culturally meaningful. They will begin to appreciate the values and ideas expressed in traditional and contemporary art. They will learn to exercise imagination, flexibility and judgement as they explore ideas and make, interpret and present artworks.

The Teacher Guide details objectives, organisation, teaching and learning approaches and evaluation and assessment guidelines. The process-based development model provides units that are organised so Learning Goals can be reinforced and expanded. Sample dialogue is incorporated into the Teaching and Learning segments to support the teaching process.

At this level children are capable of:
– working cooperatively
– expressing ideas and feelings through use of art elements
– drawing from memory, observation and imagination
– comparing and contrasting their own and others' artwork
– modifying their own work based on self-evaluation and teacher dialogue
– expressing action, emotion, beginning perspective, adding details
– building their art vocabulary
– practising new skills, working independently.

Art Eyes Book B begins with painting. Students learn how to make paintbrushes, how to make paint and how to use paintbrushes to make all kinds of lines, shapes and textures. They also learn about composition, colour, colour mixing and how colour is connected with feelings. They continue to study art through drawing with materials such as charcoal, crayon, pencil, pastel and tissue.

At Level Three or Level Four children are able to create visual art describing the illusion of space using a variety of methods. X-ray drawing is a technique where, for example, a house will appear as if one wall has disappeared and the artist draws what is inside each room.

Children also create paintings and drawings of stories using a baseline drawn across the lower horizontal edge of the paper and sometimes a skyline drawn across the upper horizontal edge making a space to place their characters or objects in between the base line and below the sky line. One of the Units has beginning perspective as its Learning Goal. This is provided to contribute to the basket of growing art knowledge that interests children at this stage of development.

The guidance and encouragement of an understanding teacher is paramount at this level for a number of reasons. Children are becoming more critical of their own work. At the same time, mathematics, writing and reading are assuming a greater significance in the overall curriculum. Teachers find art teaching more challenging within the context of an expanding general curriculum. The planning and teaching of an effective art programme demands a supportive, trusting environment for both teacher and students.

Art Eyes Book B is designed to complement **Art Eyes Book A** and present an integrated programme.

How to Use the Art Diary Pages and Teacher Guides

Teachers need to be familiar with both the Teacher Art Guide and the Art Diary pages prior to each art-making session. Most of the Art Diary pages are designed as independent study to encourage students to develop the ideas presented as part of the related Art Unit. They may be set as either homework or class work. Occasionally, students are expected to complete Art Diary assignments prior to making artworks. Reference books, computer or library access and art materials need to be made available for some Art Diary pages.

Art Words, a feature of some of the Art Diary pages, will need to be either researched by children using art texts or dictionaries or discussed in class and written on the board for students to record. Definitions for all art-related words are provided in the glossary. Reflective art time when such new language can be practised is integrated with some teaching sessions.

Learning Goals are written as part of the Teacher Guide in order to focus your assessment. When the students are made fully aware of the Learning Goals they are assisted in ongoing self-evaluation.

Italicised speech segments are provided as a guide for teachers. The teacher adopts many roles in teaching the art curriculum. These statements show how the teacher can offer specific instructional art knowledge, challenge students and guide or facilitate dialogue.

Art sessions are designed to encourage teacher-student dialogue during artmaking. This is the time when difficulties and problems may be encountered and new solutions can be successfully embraced.

The **Art Folio** referred to in a number of units can be constructed and designed as a first art project. A functional size is A2 and it may be made from manila paper or light card. The Art Folio may contain experimental draft artwork, work in progress, artwork completed outside of the classroom and artwork that is no longer on display, helping children learn to recognise their own artistic development and to value all working drawings. This collection of artwork also assists the teacher in assessment.

The **Art Shirt** can be a cut-down adult shirt or T-shirt worn to protect clothing. Acrylic paint, for example, can be washed when wet, but is permanent when dry. Diagrams assist with classroom organisation and with the introduction of new media.

Teachers are encouraged to utilise the varying interests of children to develop further units within each medium. Motivations may be sourced from the children themselves. The teacher can also find sources of motivation from common-place experiences, class trips, stories, photographs, music, shared celebrations, visitors and from the media.

Unit 18: DOT PAINTING
Plants

TIME
- 3 Sessions of 40 minutes

THEME
Dot Painting: Plants

OBJECTIVE
– interpret and communicate a visual idea

LEARNING GOALS
– explore dot painting technique
– use dots to give form to ideas and symbols
– experiment using a stick as a painting tool

MATERIALS AND RESOURCES

For each student:
- Pointed stick
- Art wipe (10 cm square cloth or paper)
- Art shirt
- White acrylic or tempera paint in plastic tray or egg carton
- Clay ball 200gm
- White cartridge paper A4
- Coloured markers

For the class:
- Plant
- Newspapers
- Bucket of water for sticks
- Stokes, Deidre *Desert Dreamings* (1993) Rigby Books

ORGANISATION

The impetus for beginning painting with an unusual tool is to develop confidence in a curriculum area where children are becoming more discerning and self-critical. There is no absolute right and wrong way to proceed with this style of painting. You will be creating an environment where children will develop the trust necessary to find visual expression for their own ideas and feelings. You will also be teaching respect for different uses of art materials and respect for cultures, past and present.

It is preferable that children either bring a stick to school or gather one from the school playground. If neither of these options exist then you will need to collect a class set of paintbrush-length sticks. For the painting session place newspapers over desks to create individual Artwork Stations.

The introductory art session sees the completion of Art Diary assignments in class after you make available texts and web sites which assist with research into **Aboriginal dot paintings**.

TEACHING AND LEARNING METHODS

SESSIONS ONE AND TWO

Western Desert acrylic dot paintings are the focus of this session to help children develop a greater understanding of why art is made. Talk about how all humans have stories of creation and laws and religious ceremonies. **Dreamtime** or Dreamings tell of the Ancestral Beings of Australian Aboriginal and Torres Strait Islander people. Ask children if they know any stories from their own cultures to tell about how the world began or how a mountain got its name.

Introduce the idea of **symbols**. Show how a dot painting uses symbols to represent real things such as land, water, people, spears and animals. Talk about how **pigment** comes from natural materials found in the earth. Ask children if they have ever tried to draw with a burnt twig from a fire or with a rough stone or brick.

Traditionally Aboriginal culture has used temporary surfaces for creating art. They have used paint on the human body, made sand paintings and created ground mosaics for sacred ceremonies.

Contemporary Aboriginal artists also work on canvas using acrylic paint.

Distribute markers and A4 white cartridge paper and set up the plant. Conceal the pot so that children draw, using only dots, just the plant coming up from the earth. All Art Diary work is completed with individual dialogues between teacher and student to assist in self-evaluation of ongoing work.

SESSION THREE

Begin the third session by asking children to share some of their dot drawings from the Art Diary and Art Folio and talk about how unique and different each drawing can be and how we each have our own secret Art Eyes to draw what we see. Cover desks with newspaper. Distribute sticks once there is an understanding that even though they are sticks and we didn't have to pay for them, they are a precious art resource and we need to use them with care.

Black cartridge paper and paint trays with white acrylic paint are passed out to each child.

You will need to demonstrate how to collect the correct quantity of paint on the stick and how to use the Art Wipe to clean off excess paint. Encourage holding the stick at different distances from the point so children can discover how best to control the paint. This will give children the opportunity to experiment with various quantities of paint on their sticks until they learn how much they require to make a small dot. Once the border is complete, invite children to use either their Art Diary drawing of a flower or their class drawing of a pot plant to create a dot painting.

ASSESSMENT/ EVALUATION

This unit fosters trust in the painting process and encourages different responses. Your Learning Goals will form the basis of your evaluation. Assess Art Diary research and drawings and comment on the growing confidence in the use of stick as a painting tool to create a visual image.

EXTENSIONS

Share reproductions and books on pointillist artists to explore together a different way to use dots. When you look at a pointillist artwork you can generally recognise what the painting represents. Artists have attempted to naturalistically represent what they see. The pointillism movement used tiny brushstrokes and dots of complementary colours to show light and shadow. Artists to look for include:

- Pisarro
- Seurat

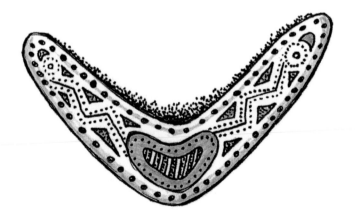

Art Diary: Dot Painting - Plants

Research

Use the Library or the Internet to find out who uses dots as a way to make paintings. Find out about Australian Aboriginal dot painting.

Art Words

Next to this list of Art Words write the definition.

DREAMTIME _____

PIGMENT _____

SYMBOL _____

List

Write the list of some of the Aboriginal language groups who live in the East Kimberley and Great Sandy Desert of Western Australia. Your teacher will provide this list and talk about the environment where the artists live.

Art Folio Artwork

Use the A4 paper your teacher provides to create a dot drawing of a potted plant using coloured markers. Keep this artwork in your Art Folio.

Drawing

Use your 6B pencil to dot an outline of a flower.

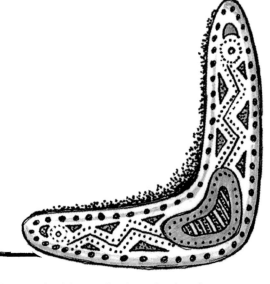

Unit 19: PAINTING
Abstract Design

Teacher Guide

TIME
- 1 Session of 30 minutes
- 1 Session of 40 minutes

THEME
Abstract Design

OBJECTIVE
– explore visual quality of paint

LEARNING GOALS
– explore and experiment with expressive qualities of paint
– look at artist's work to talk about their use of brush strokes
– gain confidence with using paint and brush

MATERIALS AND RESOURCES

For each student:
- Flathead, bristle paintbrush 2cm
- Tempera paint one colour in plastic paint tray, lid or egg carton
- Newsprint A2
- Newspaper
- Art wipe 10cm square of newspaper or cloth swatch
- Art shirt
- Coloured markers

For the class:
- Pegs on line
- Bucket for brushes
- Jars with water for brushes
- Art texts showing paintings by Gretchen Albrecht (NZ) and Morris Louis (USA)

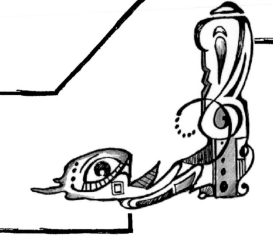

ORGANISATION

Each child stands at their desk. Cover desk with newspaper. The diagram shows a paint set-up for two children. As they will be using only one colour in this lesson sharing a paint tray works well.

Soak brushes in water prior to painting. Mix the tempera paint to a consistency of liquid detergent. This means that children can paint without using water making painting in the classroom more manageable. Show how to wipe excess paint. Soak brushes in a bucket of water at cleanup, before the final rinsing.

If you do not have paint trays for palettes collect and use plastic lids of two litre ice-cream containers. These lids make keeping colours separate more difficult but are great for mixing colours on a single surface. Recycled egg cartons can work as a substitute paint tray.

TEACHING AND LEARNING METHODS

SESSION ONE

This session explores the **linear** quality of lines. Explain how standing up helps us see the space we have to paint in, which means we make better judgements about making shapes in the whole space. Ask children how they think they can use their paintbrush. Refer to Dot Painting Art Unit.

Introduce the term **magic paintbrush**. Here the child holds their imaginary paintbrush in the air to make imaginary lines and shapes.

Take the "magic paintbrush" and drag it slowly through the air. Make car tyre tracks. Practise long smooth lines. Practise jerky, sharp lines. Make lines with curves and lines with hard angles. Make dots and dashes.

Have children take their "magic paintbrush" for a walk and hold it like a pencil to control lines and paint small careful edges of lines and shapes.

Introduce Art Diary work and use the rest of this session to complete the Investigation, Drawing and Writing assignments. Provide coloured markers.

SESSION TWO

Take the "magic paintbrush" for a long peaceful walk in the air. Explain how to drag a paintbrush smoothly around the newsprint making five closed curves. You may need to demonstrate how much paint can be absorbed by a flathead paintbrush to avoid drips. Distribute paint and paintbrushes that have been soaked in water.

Once their long uninterrupted line painting is complete paintbrushes are laid down on the work surface. Now is the time to choose a different line. In each of the closed curves they will make a series of different lines.

Take the "magic paintbrush" through various explorations such as a steep path, a crooked path, a bumpy road, a winding road, a pot-holed road, a straight and narrow path, a maze, a zigzag line, a wee road, a four-lane motorway.

Ask children to think about ways they can use their fat paintbrush to make thin lines, talk about using the tip of the paintbrush, stippling, swerving, holding the brush lightly, pressing carefully. Ask what happens when a line is repeated in the same space. Talk about how patterns are made through the use of repetition.

This artwork will be pegged to dry before going into their Art Folios. This artwork is experimental and is designed to give young artists confidence in painting. Share artworks by local and international abstract artists.

ASSESSMENT AND EVALUATION

These are foundation artmaking sessions where you will be providing an opportunity for children to develop painting skills. Observe growing confidence with brushstrokes and understandings of line and pattern. Have children refer to this experimental work when they are looking for solutions in future painting work.

Art Diary: Painting Abstract Design

Imagine

Imagine that one day you woke up and you were a paintbrush! Here are some tasks for you.

Writing

What are some of the paintings you will paint now that you are a paintbrush? What kinds of brushstrokes will you make?

Draw

Draw a fast line. Draw a jumping line. Draw a swimming line. Draw a cold line. Draw a smooth line. Draw a furry line.

Unit 20: PAINTING
Sea Anemone

TIME
- 2 Sessions of 40 minutes

THEME
Sea Anemone

OBJECTIVES
– explore and experiment with colour
– express visual ideas

LEARNING GOALS
– mix colours to gain understanding of properties of colours
– use primary colours to create imaginary sea anemones
– experiment with textural application of paint
– practise overlapping

MATERIALS AND RESOURCES

For each student:
- Acrylic primary colours in plastic paint tray
- Sponge for each colour
- Cartridge paper A3
- Newsprint A4
- Newspaper
- Peg for each colour
- Art shirt

For the class:
- Bucket for sponges
- Bucket of warm soapy water
- Paper towels
- Plastic tarpaulin or mat

ORGANISATION

One of the reasons painting becomes a challenge for teachers at Level 3 and Level 4 is the demands of other curriculum areas, often resulting in a lesser role for the visual arts. Hence many classroom layouts add an extra burden to teaching visual art. Some schools are able to set up a separate spare room which makes set up and cleanup less time-consuming. The diagram shows children seated on a tarpaulin or plastic sheeting with paint trays and pegged sponges.

TEACHING AND LEARNING METHODS

SESSION ONE

Provide photographs and books and web sites for Art Diary research. Introduce the concepts of **primary colours** and **secondary colours** by inviting children to describe the colours they see in the classroom. Ask if anyone knows what happens when you mix red and blue. Work through the List project in the Art Diary using pastels to discover the secondary colours. Keep these experimental artworks in the Art Folio. Distribute paint trays, sponges and pegs. Ask each child to make two blobs of yellow and one blob of blue. Add red to blue and yellow. Add blue to yellow. Ask what colours are slowly being mixed. Practise shapes and more colour mixing.

Ask if any child speaks another language. Ask if any child knows the words for red, yellow and blue. If not, set out to discover this together and write on the board.

Complete the Research, Drawing and Poem Art Diary assignments in this session.

SESSION TWO

Talk about how children will be painting one large sea anemone surrounded by smaller sea anemones that are hiding most of their shape behind the large anemone. Read Art Diary poems aloud. Invite three children to sketch on the board how they radiated lines from the centre of their sea anemone. Talk about **texture**. Ask them to describe the texture of their own hair. What does that feel like?

Start to paint using clean clear primary colours and then blend the colours to make secondary colours. Explain that the use of a sponge as a painting tool will help create a texture we desire for our sea anemones.

"Start with a large sea anemone in the middle of your page. Leave enough room for a few other anemones. Paint to fill the whole page. Can you hide some of the small sea anemones behind your large central sea anemone?"

Select individual paintings to discuss during artmaking. Ask who can see examples of overlapping? Talk about the kinds of textures painted. Encourage full use of the paper. Peg up examples of work that show good use of space. These will be helpful for others. Ask them what they see first when looking at an individual painting.

ASSESSMENT AND EVALUATION

Art Diary work allows for analysis of individual understanding of primary and secondary colours. The process of mixing paint, the textural possibilities of sponge application and development of visual ideas will be evident in the artwork. At all times the context of Art Words contributes to a growing knowledge of both media and visual ideas. Taking time to interact during artmaking sessions allows for ongoing evaluations for the students. New solutions can be found and new directions followed after constructive talking, observing and listening.

EXTENSIONS

When the paintings are dry students may use black and white crayon to highlight and outline individual anemones.

Art Diary: Painting Sea Anemone

Research

Investigate photographs of wildflowers and sea anemones. Look carefully at colours.

List

List the secondary colours.
What colour do you get when you mix:
• red and blue?.........................
• red and yellow?......................
• blue and yellow?......................

List

List the primary colours in two more languages.

English		
RED		
BLUE		
YELLOW		

Poem

Write a poem using the names of all the primary colours.

Invention

Invent words to describe colours you see in your home. For example, bubble-gum pink or skate-board grey.

Drawing

Draw an imaginary sea anemone.

Unit 21: PAINTING
Colour and Feelings

TIME

• 3 Sessions of 40 minutes

THEME

Colour and Feelings

OBJECTIVE

– express personal feelings, emotions and sensations

LEARNING GOALS

– express feelings with colours

– use line and shape and colour to paint a human figure

– understand terms such as shade and tint

– use harmonious colours

MATERIALS AND RESOURCES

For each student:
• Viewfinder art frame
• Brush 2 cm
• Child chooses one acrylic colour plus white and a dot of black*
• Newspapers
• Art wipe (10cm square cloth swatch or newspaper)
• Art shirt
• Cartridge white paper A3
• Scissors
• Oil pastels, harmonious colours
* One space is left in paint tray for water.

For the class:
• Bucket of water for brushes
• Recycled plastic water containers
• Comic books popular with this age group

ORGANISATION

Once the colour has been selected, set out paint in trays near the painting surface. Ideally children should stand to do this painting, either at their individual Artwork Stations or at groups of desks. Ensure you have the most comfortable arrangement organised for painting so that you are able to walk around to observe and interact with individuals during the painting process.

Brushes are soaked in jars of water prior to distribution. Art Wipes are used to squeeze excess paint between colour use. Explain that the water in their paint trays, is to be used carefully to dilute the primary colour. Encourage cleaning of the brush by using the Art Wipe. Brushes are delivered to a bucket of water to soak before a thorough clean and dry at the end of the third session.

The Viewfinder Art Frame is an essential tool for this painting session and it helps to contain exactly what we see and what we will paint. It consists of a 10 cm square piece of card which has a 2cm square cut out in the middle to provide a gap to look through and frame what you are seeing, much like a window frame.

TEACHING AND LEARNING METHODS

SESSION ONE

Talk about how colour can represent feelings. For example, ask students what colour they think of when they are happy. Introduce Art Diary Writing and Drawing assignments. Invite them to share their responses to the Writing project. Ask one child to model how they pose when they are feeling tired and sleepy. Complete Art Diary work.

SESSION TWO

One child can choose positions and facial expressions to show a variety of emotions. Students can hold their Viewfinder Art Frames to see how a body can contain **curves** and **angles**. Use a Viewfinder Art Frame to experiment with various viewpoints such as birds-eye, close up, frontal and profile.

"Use your "magic paintbrush" to outline the shape of Julie.
How round is her head? What can you see of her whole body?
Is she looking frightened? Is she looking excited? Does she
seem to look bigger when she is excited? Does she seem to look
tiny when she is afraid?"

Comic books can be used to show how comic artists constantly change the viewpoint for the viewer and reader. Talk about feelings. How small or large do you feel when you are happy or angry? Different people perceive colours and objects differently.

Re-visit different ways to hold a paintbrush to achieve different kinds of shapes and lines. Encourage children to feel confident about expressing different emotions and explain how each painting will look very different.

Once children have chosen the feeling they wish to paint add the chosen colour to the paint tray that already holds white and a little dot of black. They now paint a human figure using both shape and colour to express emotion.

Introduce the word **shade** for when you add a little black to make a colour darker. Introduce the word **tint** to show how to start with white and add a little colour to make a lighter colour. Demonstrate how you always begin with white to make a tint then add the colour. When you add white or a little black to a colour this is called a **tone**.

SESSION THREE

As we are interested in the emotional value of colour and shape the background will not be painted. Talk about details they can add or how to highlight their painting. Help children identify one harmonious colour for their pastel work. Distribute scissors and assist where necessary to cut around their figure paintings. Display together as a group.

ASSESSMENT AND EVALUATION

Evaluation of colour choice and composition can be done through discussion, Art Diary reading and observation of painting. The children will be building on their knowledge and dexterity with paint and brushes to create line, shape and colour mixing to make shades, tints and tones. However the focus of the assessment will be the use of colour to convey feeling. Ask what happened when they added a harmonious colour in oil pastel. Invite individuals to reflect on their paintings.

Make use of your school's art print collection and show an artist's work to help children appreciate the relationship between their own art and the wider world of art.

ART DIARY: PAINTING COLOUR AND FEELINGS

WRITING

What colours do you choose when you are painting to show the feeling of:

- happiness...?_____
- loneliness...?_____
- anger....?_____
- peacefulness...?_____
- curiosity....?_____

ART WORDS

Next to this list of Art Words write the definition.

ANGLE _____

CURVE _____

SHADE _____

TINT _____

TONE _____

DRAWING

Choose a coloured marker and draw a picture saying "I am sleepy".

Choose a coloured marker to draw a picture with a title: "My hands are freezing cold".

WRITE

Name one colour that is in harmony with red. _____

Name one colour that is in harmony with blue. _____

Name one colour that is in harmony with yellow. _____

Unit 22: PAINTING
Portraits/Profiles

TIME
- 3 Sessions of 40 minutes

THEME
Portraits/
Profiles

OBJECTIVE
− respond to personal and sensory experiences to create artworks

LEARNING GOALS
− build on previous painting knowledge to create a portrait and a profile
− use shades and tints and experiment with texture
− use light and dark tones to describe three-dimensional form
− use photographs as source of motivation for painting

MATERIALS AND RESOURCES

For each student:
- Paint in plastic tray or on plastic lid - two primary colours plus black and white
- 1 brush 2cm
- 1 brush 1cm
- Art wipe
- Art shirt
- 6B pencil
- Newspaper
- Cartridge paper A3 x 2

For the class:
- Bucket of water for clean-up of brushes
- Torch
- Paste
- Newspapers and magazines
- Plastic recycled containers for water (optional)
- Photographic art books
- Egyptian art images

ORGANISATION

Bring photography books to class and/or a visit a photographic exhibition.

If you wish to have children clean brushes between colours with water your setup will require access to small containers of water.

The children can, however, carefully use an Art Wipe to clean the brush between colours. This process causes fewer mishaps in a class setting. At the end of the session children place used brushes in the water bucket.

TEACHING AND LEARNING METHODS

SESSION ONE

Visit an exhibition of contemporary photography or invite an artist to visit the class so that your students have the opportunity to explore the way photography provides a means of artistic expression. Newspapers and magazines can be used to show the documentary and commercial nature of photography.

Invite children to bring **photographs** they like, to share with the class. Ask why people take photographs. Ask them to talk about what makes a photograph interesting. Ask them to think about what the photographer is attempting to portray.

Complete Art Words and Drawing assignments.

SESSION TWO

Invite children to use their "magic paintbrush" to trace in the air the contour of one student's profile. Help them see how a nose looks from the side. You can show how the Egyptians painted to include all features even when they were painting in profile.

Talk about how we are using our Art Eyes to paint what we see. Talk about how to first add a dot of black to slowly darken a colour. Remind children how to add colour to white to make a lighter tone. Revisit tint and shade. Invite a parent or colleague to be the model so that you are free to roam during the painting session to help develop knowledge of shade and tint.

Introduce the word **caricature** and explain that it can be comical to exaggerate features, but that today we are trying to draw what we see. Use the first piece of A3 so children may paint a profile.

SESSION THREE

How light falls on a subject can best be presented in class by darkening the room and using a single light source such as a torch to glow on a subject. Invite one child to sit so that the light shines directly onto the front of the face. Next, shine the torch on one side of the face. In each case, ask children what they notice about the features. Where is the face dark? Where is the face light?

Make reference to their first painting of a profile to see how successfully different children used paint to show tones. Evaluation during the artmaking assists individual choices prior to completion of artwork. Encourage full use of the paper by outlining the face with one colour at first.

ASSESSMENT AND EVALUATION

This lesson builds on the growing knowledge of painting. The role of photography in contemporary art is presented to encourage children to think about different kinds of visual images. Use of shades and tints to create a portrait and a profile will be assessed. Understanding and using a budding art vocabulary can be noted both in conversation during motivation time and in artmaking.

EXTENSION

Use one roll of black-and-white film to take each child's portrait. Once printed, the image is photocopied and enlarged. Students can use oil pastels to add naturalistic colour.

ART DIARY: PAINTING – PORTRAITS / PROFILES

RESEARCH

Look through old magazines and newspapers for photographs of people.

ART WORDS

Next to this list of Art Words write the definition.

PROFILE _____

PORTRAIT _____

PHOTOGRAPH _____

CUT AND PASTE

Cut out two small (about 5cm x 5cm) photographs of heads of people. Choose one where the person is facing the camera and you can see the whole face. Choose one profile. Paste each picture in one of these boxes.

DRAWING

In the box next to the photograph use your 6B pencil to redraw the face. What is clearly outlined? What is in shadow? Look carefully to see the curves of the nose and mouth and eyes.

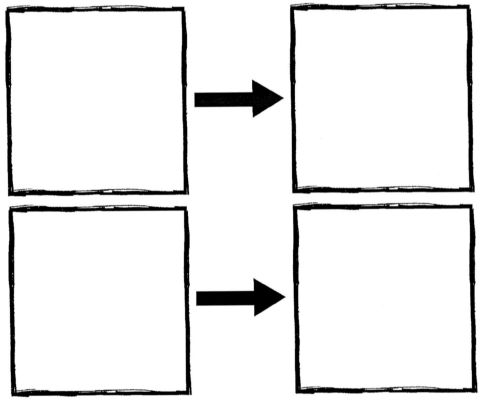

WRITING

Choose one portrait and write what you think the person is feeling or thinking about. Is the person feeling happy? Or are they sad? How can you tell?

RESEARCH

Look through the photography books your teacher has brought to the class.

Unit 23: COLLAGE
Tivaevae Flower

Teacher Guide

TIME

• 2 Sessions of 40 minutes and 1 of 20 minutes

THEME

Tivaevae Flower

OBJECTIVE

– introduce recent Eastern Polynesian tivaevae tradition to help students examine the significance of art making in past and present cultures

LEARNING GOALS

– understand the tivaevae process and the way quilts are made and valued within a community

– create a symmetrical design based on natural forms

– select and arrange collage elements to create a composition

– learn about complementary or contrasting colours

MATERIALS AND RESOURCES

For each student:
• White card 20cm x 20cm
• 6 coloured papers 10cm x 10cm
• 6 coloured papers 10cm x 10cm
• PVA paste in glue bottle
• Scissors*
• Art shirt
• Paper towel
* Only use scissors where safety and competency allow

For the class:
• Prism
• Tivaevae quilt
• Plastic tarpaulin or mat
• Hammond, J. *Tifaifai and Quilts of Polynesia* (1986) University of Hawaii Press
• Robertson,A. *Patterns of Polynesia — The Cook Islands* (1989) Heinemann Education
• Rongea, L. *Tivaevae, Portraits of Cook Island Quilting* (1992) Daphne Brasell Associates

ORGANISATION

Bring a tivaevae quilt to school or books with tivaevae patterns and flowers. Visit flowers growing in the playground or flowers in the class. This unit can be linked to a science unit on planting seeds or studying flowers.

Children share a working space with a plastic tarpaulin on the floor. Coloured paper can be placed centrally as each child will need to choose three colours for each artwork. Paste can be set out for each child. Go through the Art Diary activities first.

TEACHING AND LEARNING METHODS

SESSION ONE

Tivaevae is a technique of quilting and stitching in cotton fabric. It is an art form developed from the introduction of appliqué quilting to some Pacific islands (such as the Hawaiian and the Cooks). It is often a collective artwork. Here children will work as a group seated on the floor. Their individual tivaevae will be connected to other collages to make one large bedspread-size artwork.

You are fortunate if you are part of a Polynesian community where the children can observe at first hand the tivaevae process and talk with artists creating their tivaevae. If you are relying on reproduced images, point out how simple shapes are repeated to create patterns and motifs of flowers and plants are common. Ask why they imagine flowers are used as a motif. Ask why flowers are considered to be beautiful. If a flower has no perfume, what else makes it beautiful?

Instead of fabric, children will use torn paper to make their tivaevae pattern. First they choose colours from the same family, harmonious colours to make their first torn paper **collage**. For example they could choose blue, blue-green and blue-violet. Or they could choose orange, red-orange and yellow-orange. Note how the subtle harmonious colour changes create a unified, calm composition.

Show how the first layer of torn paper is glued to the card to provide the **background** colour. If this is the first time children are using paste, you may need to demonstrate how little paste needs to be put on the torn and cut paper to successfully glue the design. Tear two similar shades of one colour to make the next two layers. Aim for petal shapes.

Ask children for ideas so they can make designs symmetrical. Experiment with laying out torn petals in different patterns. Use a piece of a paper towel to wipe any excess glue and remind children to use glue sparingly.

SESSION TWO

For the second session choose complementary colours to **cut** a second tivaevae flower collage. Complementary colours can create a dynamic composition as they are sharply different from each other, for example: orange and blue, yellow and violet, red and green. Talk about how the eye seems to jump from colour to colour. Distribute scissors, glue, coloured paper and card.

SESSION THREE

Use a 20 minute reflection time to invite comments on the art process and tivaevae creation. If the day is sunny, now is the time to use a **prism** to talk about colour and to develop knowledge of colour as a visual element. Use particular examples of student artwork to reinforce understanding. Glue art works to create two large tivaevae collages. Use children's suggestions to create these designs.

ASSESSMENT AND EVALUATION

Observe creativity and discernment in choosing colours. Assess composition and understanding of tivaevae process.

Art Diary: Collage Tivaevae Flower

Research

In Polynesia, one of the most important traditional arts is tivaevae or quiltmaking.

Use books in the classroom and in the Library to look at tivaevae patterns. There are different styles and patterns among the Pacific Islands. Look at tivaevae from the Cook Islands, Society Islands and Hawaiian Islands.

Design

Design your own tivaevae pattern in this square divided into four. Draw a simple petal shape in each square to create a symmetrical pattern. Use bright colours to help your pattern stand out.

Art Words

Next to this list of Art Words write the definition.

BACKGROUND _____

HUE _____

PRISM _____

TIVAEVAE _____

COLLAGE _____

List

List the colours or hues of the rainbow.

R _____

O _____

Y _____

G _____

B _____

I _____

V _____

Write

Write the name of one colour that is complementary or opposite to:

Green _____

Orange _____

Violet _____

Write

Complete these sentences.

The opposite of smooth is _____

The opposite of fast is _____

The opposite of curved is _____

Unit 24: SGRAFFITO
Celebrations

TIME

- 3 Sessions of 60 minutes

THEME

Celebrations

OBJECTIVE

– show inventive use of materials

LEARNING GOALS

– create a sgraffito drawing

– respond imaginatively to a celebratory event

MATERIALS AND RESOURCES

For each student:
- Wax crayons, light and bright colours only
- Black thick tempera paint
- Flat-head large paintbrush 3cm
- Cartridge paper A3
- Newspapers
- Paper clip folded open
- Art shirt
- 2B pencil

For the class:
- Bucket of water
- 3cm strips of white paper for frame
- Scissors
- Newspapers or tarpaulin

ORGANISATION

Sgraffito is an art process that uses black paint over crayon to provide a surface that can be scratched to reveal the colours of the wax crayons under the dark surface.

A thick wad of newspaper is distributed to each child to provide a soft surface on which to place the cartridge paper. This simple setup makes it easier to strongly press crayons in order to achieve a solid bright mass of colour.

Black paint is best set up at the teacher Artwork Station so that covering the bright crayon work can take place here. Once work is painted lay it flat to dry. Cover the floor space with either newspapers or a tarpaulin.

This work is best displayed against a pale background.

TEACHING AND LEARNING METHODS

SESSION ONE

Ask students to close their eyes and imagine a colourful celebration they may have seen in real life or on television. Complete the Art Diary Research and Writing assignments. The Drawing assignment will be referred to in Session Three. Ask for ideas about how to capture the effects of fireworks.

SESSION TWO

Children write their own name on the back of the paper using a 2B pencil. Talk about the process of sgraffito, how bright crayon is covered in black and then designs are scratched through the black paint. Explain how to use the point and the side of the crayons to cover the whole paper with intense colour. Show how to press heavily with crayons or pastels to achieve the depth of colour needed so that the bright colours of celebration will shine through.

SESSION THREE

The third session can begin with distributing the now black artworks and the folded out paper clips. Children scrape designs with paper clips or other fine-tipped objects they may find such as sharp small twigs. Talk about contrast so that children can make good decisions regarding how much black remains on the surface of their final artwork. Ideas for shapes include stars, bright lights, flags, food or people.

Invite children who complete work early to crayon 3 cm wide strips of white paper with firework patterns to make simple borders for the finished work so that you can staple into the wall a pre-designed and reuseable set of frames for work of this size.

ASSESSMENT AND EVALUATION

Prior to selection of paper size you will know the array of skills in your class. You may choose to have children work on paper half the suggested size. Observe each child's ability to press the crayons into the surface to achieve bright colours throughout the scraped final artwork. Art Diary work will show you the extent of their understanding of why people celebrate. Contrast between light and bright is the skill you can assess once the work is complete.

ART DIARY: SGRAFFITO CELEBRATIONS

RESEARCH
Use library books or the Internet to find out about celebrations in two cultures.

DRAWING
Use coloured markers to draw yourself dressed up to celebrate. What colours and shapes will make it a special celebration. Give your drawing a title.

TITLE:

WRITING
Write the names and dates of the celebrations you have discovered on the back of this paper.

Unit 25: PAINTING AND COLLAGE
Myth - Rata and His Canoe

TIME

- 3 Sessions of 40 minutes or one whole morning

THEME

Myth - Rata and His Canoe

OBJECTIVES

– explore the relationship between two media to develop visual ideas
– develop and apply understanding of properties of colour

LEARNING GOALS

– create artwork in collage and paint
– develop dexterity in use of brush to add details
– use imagination and visual ideas to tell part of a story
– learn Maori names for different insects, birds and trees, such as:
  kereru, kowhai, manuka, piwakawaka, rimu, ruru, totara, tui, weta

MATERIALS AND RESOURCES

For each student:

- Tempera paint primary colours, plus white and a dot of black in plastic tray
- 1 brush 1cm
- 1 brush 2cm
- Cartridge A2
- Art shirt
- Art wipe
- Newspaper
- PVA paste in squeeze plastic bottle
- Scissors
- 4B pencil
- Plastic ice-cream lid palette

For the class:

- Plastic recycled containers for water
- Brushes, spare
- Bucket water
- MacDonald, R. *Nga Korero a Nga Tamariki* (1996) Lands End
- School Journal Part 1, # 4 1981, Rata's Canoe. Learning Media

ORGANISATION

Begin with storytelling and role-playing. Second session is collage and completion of Art Diary work. Use a combination of cut and torn newsprint to collage the tree trunk shapes. The third session is painting. Paint is set out in plastic paint tray, one for each child.

Familiarise yourself with the story of Rata until you are able to tell the story.

TEACHING AND LEARNING METHODS

SESSION ONE

Tell the story of *Rata and His Canoe*. You can retell the story with children role-playing prior to painting.

Imagine if you didn't have enough to eat. What could be done? Rata lives near the sea. His family is hungry. They have gathered berries and fruits. They have gathered shellfish like pipi and tuatua, but all the fish seem to live out to sea. One thing Rata doesn't have is a canoe.

One day he enters the forest. He finds a tall wide tree.

"This will be perfect for a canoe," he smiles to himself.

He begins work chopping and chopping until after a very long day the tree falls. Rata is exhausted. He decides to go home to sleep. He will return tomorrow to carve the canoe.

While Rata is sleeping, all the birds and insects pick up all the wood shavings and join the tree together so that when Rata returns he is astonished to see the tree is standing right where he saw it yesterday morning before he began all his hard work.

There is nothing else to be done. He starts work all over and at nightfall he returns home to sleep. When he goes back to the forest the tree is standing once more. He is very puzzled. So after spending the whole day, once again, cutting and chopping he decides not to go home. He will rest, with his ears wide open, right here in the forest and hide behind a low bush.

Rata rests awhile until he hears the fantail chirping and the huhu grub slithering. He jumps out from behind the bush and is startled to see all the insects and birds working to gather wood chips.

"Why are you undoing all my hard work?" he asks.

The birds and insects all begin to talk at the same time and he can't understand a word. Slowly it becomes clear to him that he has failed to say a karakia or prayer to Tane God of the Forest to ask permission to cut down the totara, which is one of Tane's children.

Rata is very sad that he has offended Tane. The birds and insects see how unhappy and sorry he is so they teach him a karakia. Rata then speaks his prayer to Tane in the forest. He is still very tired from his work so he lies down and rests. While he is resting the birds and insects peck and nibble and chomp until the canoe is carved with beautiful decorations.

Children take various roles such as insects, birds, trees and Rata and his family so that each child has the opportunity to perform as you re-tell *Rata and His Canoe*. Art Diary work begins, including Writing assignments.

SESSION TWO

This session involves the creation and completion of collage work. Remind children of how they learned to do collage with their tivaevae unit. For this unit students will use newspaper to cut out shapes of trees and shrubs such as the tall totara and dense manuka. Hand out scissors. Experiment with moving cut shapes of trees and shrubs all over the cartridge paper to create a satisfying composition. Distribute PVA paste and remind children to apply a small amount of paste to each cut shape.

The forest will be cut and pasted during this art session. Use 4B pencil to add names of children to each artwork on the reverse. Complete Art Diary work.

SESSION THREE

Distribute larger brushes and paints. Encourage the use of the large paintbrush for big shapes and colour application to trees and background. Hand out the smaller paintbrush when students are ready to add details such as leaves, birds, insects or Rata.

All the colours they need should be squeezed into their paint tray. Remind students to wipe brushes clean between colours. Distribute spare paintbrushes where necessary or ask children to use water to help with cleaning brushes or thinning a colour. Encourage use of the whole page to show how big the forest is.

ASSESSMENT AND EVALUATION

Use of paintbrushes to add detail will be a focus of this assessment. Observation of painting skills and developing visual imagination may be noted through the lesson and on completion of artwork. Developing composition skills using both collage and paint should be observable. Use class time to have children reflect on the learning processes. Ask students to comment on their choice of subject matter, specific techniques such as creating light and dark areas, colour mixing and the addition of details.

EXTENSION

Story motivations of myths and legends from around the world can be used to develop painting and collage techniques so that your painting programme extends through a term. If you have a computer in the classroom encourage the development of painting techniques.

Art Diary: Painting and Collage – Myth

RESEARCH

Visit the Library. Find a book on Mythologies.

Find one book on Polynesian sea voyagers. Look at how they travelled.

Find a book on native trees from your homeland.

ART WORDS

Look at the insect, bird and tree names you have learned to recognise in Maori. Write what each one is.

KERERU _____

KOWHAI _____

PIWAKAWAKA _____

RURU _____

TOTARA _____

TUI _____

WETA _____

WRITING

Write down the titles of two myths and the countries they are from.

_____   _____

_____   _____

DRAWING

Draw a voyaging canoe in this space.

Rewrite the story of *Rata and His Canoe* in your own words on separate paper.

WRITING

Write a short poem about one of the trees that are indigenous to your land.

Unit 26: PAINTING
Myth - Maui Catching the Sun

Teacher Guide

TIME

- 2 Sessions of 60 minutes

THEME

Myth - Maui Catching the Sun

OBJECTIVE

– generate imaginary and naturalistic representations in response to story motivation

LEARNING GOALS

– explore the qualities of paint such as: colour, line, shape, space, and texture
– listen creatively to the telling of a myth from Maori cultural tradition

MATERIALS AND RESOURCES

For each student:

- Acrylic or tempera paint in plastic trays. Primary, mixed colours and black and white
- 1 brush 2cm
- 1 brush 1cm
- Newspaper
- White cartridge paper A2 sheet
- Art shirt

For the class:

- Woven articles such as baskets or kete
- Polyurethane spray if using tempera paint

ORGANISATION

Prior to this lesson organise a display area for the work either in the class or in a public area in the school, such as the foyer or library. Each painting will have one or two descriptive sentences to assist the viewer. Set up paint trays for each child. You will only need to use polyurethane spray if the children use tempera paint, as it dries dull or matte. Use this spray outside, as the fumes are toxic.

TEACHING AND LEARNING METHODS

SESSION ONE

Practise the story of *Maui Catching the Sun* until you can tell the story without reference to the printed word. It can be a very simple re-telling.

A long, long time ago when the earth was much younger Maui and his family found themselves working very quickly. Why? The sun was racing across the sky.

Maui asks the sun to slow down so that his people in Aotearoa can have enough time to plant and dance and carve before darkness arrives. The sun turns up his nose. He refuses to slow down.

Maui has an idea. Many women are skilled basket weavers. Maui asks all the people to cut leaves from the harakeke, flax bush. They strip the leaf of its spine and edges. After softening the long green strips Maui asks all the men and women to weave long ropes with a net at one end.

What is Maui going to do with the long ropes? He wants to catch the sun. He carries the rope and net to the edge where the sun comes up in the morning. He wants to surprise the sun. Just as the sun appears in the sky Maui throws the woven net around the sun.

The sun struggles to be free. He asks Maui what he wants. Maui says, "All I would like is for you to slow down as you cross the sky so my people can have time to work and play before night falls."

The sun agrees and to this day we have time to plant food, to catch fish, to go to school, all before the sun disappears from our horizon."

Complete Art Diary Writing and Memory Drawing assignments.

SESSION TWO

Re-tell the myth with children acting various roles. Now that you have developed a pattern of engaging with children during the art process you will find opportunities to aid and guide the composition. Talk about using the whole page. Suggest ways to represent aspects of the story so that when all artworks are complete your exhibition will tell most of the tale.

Encourage use of the large paintbrush to paint flowing large lines such as the rope as it is tossed, or the speeding sun. Decide what or who will be in the **foreground** and what will be happening in the background. Hand out the smaller brush to encourage the addition of details such as the **texture** of woven rope.

Horizontal baselines and skylines or X-ray techniques will show how various students use space. Telling the story is paramount. Your input as you circulate can reference how colour can make us have certain feelings toward a subject such as:

"If we want to show how angry and upset the sun is feeling what colours shall we choose? If we want to show how quickly darkness overtakes the day how do we paint a dark tone?"

You may choose to create a third Art Session to complete the artwork and invite students to write a description of their paintings for the exhibition.

ASSESSMENT AND EVALUATION

Observe and interact during the art process and try to take a few notes. You will comment on use of space and the addition of details. Always take time to discuss the Learning Goals in a way that help children to understand your expectations. This assists in self-evaluation as well as your assessment.

Organise Art Partners to be Art Guides once the exhibition is on display. Over a period of a week children can assist viewers for 10 minutes at playtime or lunchtime.

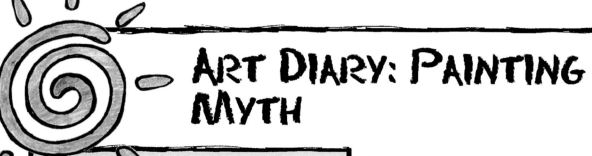

ART DIARY: PAINTING MYTH

RESEARCH

How do people look when they are running? Find some photographs in old magazines or newspapers to see how people look when they are moving quickly.

ART WORDS

Next to this list of Art Words write the definition.

FOREGROUND _____

WEAVING _____

TEXTURE _____

READING

Visit the library and read some myths. Remember which countries the stories are from.

MEMORY DRAWING

Sketch, from memory, your idea of how you look when you are running.

WRITING

Write the titles of the stories you have read and the countries they are from.

-
-
-
-

Re-tell the story of *Maui Catching the Sun*. Use your own words on separate paper.

Unit 27: CAVE ART AND ROCK PAINTING
Wild Animals

TIME
• 2 Sessions of 50 minutes or one whole morning

THEME
Wild Animals

OBJECTIVE
– appreciate how painting has been used for different purposes in history

LEARNING GOALS
– grate brick dust and mix in animal fat to make paint
– fray a twig to make a paintbrush
– use charcoal and paint to create a wild animal design on newspaper and textured paper
– research cave drawings and petroglyphs to generate visual ideas

MATERIALS AND RESOURCES

For each student:
• Newspapers
• Art shirt
• Old soft bricks, broken bricks, sufficient for each student to have two hand-size pieces
• Stick or twig for extra brush
• Charcoal
• 1 recycled textured wallpaper cut to A4
• Old rasps

For the class:
• Electric frying pan
• Kitchen ladle
• Small recycled tins
• Bucket of warm soapy water
• Animal fat

ORGANISATION

The first session requires newspaper spread over the floor. This is the working surface. Brick dust is made by rubbing a small piece of brick against another brick. Each child grates the bricks onto a folded whole newspaper segment so that when dust is collected into the recycled tin it will easily slide down the fold.

The second session requires the teacher to heat fat, either in an electric frying pan or double boiler. Once this is melted and before it cools, it is ladled onto the brick dust in the tin cans. While the fat is melting children use charcoal twigs or lumps from the sawdust firing (see Sawdust Firing Unit in Book A.) Prepare twig paintbrushes by applying pressure to one end to fray fibres.

Brick fragments, twigs, newspapers and charcoal can be brought from home.

TEACHING AND LEARNING METHODS

SESSION ONE

Complete the Art Diary work before the first session so that students will already have looked at images of ancient rock art from Australia, Spain, France and Aotearoa/New Zealand. Raise questions about how artists worked, what their subject matter was and why they painted.

Session one is hard work for everyone. It requires patience and time to create the brick dust you need for the painting session. You will know your class and be able to judge what length of time makes sense for this session. You will probably have sufficient brick dust after 30 minutes of rasping and grating.

This is collective work and all brick dust is gathered into one container ready for re-distribution into smaller cans shared between two for painting in the next session. Cleanup, followed by children running around the playground shouting at the top of their lungs is the best way to end this intense artwork session!

SESSION TWO

If you do not want to take a whole morning to complete the entire Unit, begin the second session by asking students to refer to their research. Use images from reference books to look at the different kinds of cave and rock art. They will sketch a draft design of a wild animal on newspaper using a charcoal lump. The design can be a creature or an abstract design. While this artwork is underway, heat the animal fat ready to ladle into the tin cans.

After you have discussed their draft designs, students charcoal their designs on the blank side of the textured wallpaper. Discuss how bumpy the texture of a real cave or rock surface would be. Explain that the wallpaper is our "rock surface".

Twigs are now frayed by pressing a fragment of brick against one end of the twig. Fingers may also be used as a method of applying paint. Sharing one tin can of brick dust mixed with animal fat between two is ideal. Painting is completed and charcoal touches can be added to help add strength and rhythm to designs.

ASSESSMENT AND EVALUATION

Set aside a separate time to encourage reflection on the learning process. Use this occasion and the observation of the artmaking to assess your learning goals and objective. As with other learning areas, you will want to bring available books on the subject into the class and allow class time for research. This will make research more egalitarian depending on your students' access to books and the Internet at home. Evaluating a student's understanding of how some art materials can be made and how there can be a variety of purposes for artmaking comes from class discussion, Art Diary work and class participation in the creation of materials.

Art Diary: Cave Art and Rock Painting – Wild Animals

RESEARCH

People have researched and come up with various ideas about why people paint. Some of the ideas are: to create magic, to try to capture the spirit of an animal, to record stories of hunting. Use the library or internet to find out about cave art in Spain, France, Australia and Aotearoa/New Zealand.

ART WORDS

Next to this list of Art Words write the definitions.

PETROGLYPH _____

PIGMENT   _____

WRITING

Write a story about how you discover rock drawings in your own area. What do you feel like when you find art made by someone long ago? Describe the designs. Are they of canoes or humans or birds?

DRAWING

Use your pencil to sketch a cave drawing similar to those in the caves found by a school-girl in Altamira, Spain.

Imagine the drawings you might find on a cave wall. Draw your own cave art.

52

Unit 28: OIL PASTELS
Skies

TIME
• 4 Sessions of 40 minutes

THEME
Skies

OBJECTIVE
– show how to communicate a visual idea

LEARNING GOALS
– learn to blend colours
– explore expressive qualities of crayon media
– create compositions using warm and cool colours toexpress feelings

MATERIALS AND RESOURCES

For each student:
• Viewfinder art frame
• Art shirt
• 6B pencil
• Red, yellow, orange, blue, green, violet, white and black oil pastels
• White cartridge paper A3 x 2
• White cartridge paper A4

For the class:
• Art books and reproductions of Impressionist artists such as Turner and Monet
• Paper towels
• Bucket of warm soapy water

ORGANISATION

Make sure the Art Shirt covers all clothing. Oil pastel stains are difficult to remove from fabric. Place a wad of newspaper underneath each student's art paper to create a slightly absorbent surface. This assists with oil pastel application to give density of colour.

Demonstrate how heavily students need to push their oil pastel to achieve a solid colour. Make sure the newspaper is larger than the drawing paper. You want to see the oil pastel bleeding off the cartridge and onto the newspaper so that the full page is used. Use the shiny surface of the white cartridge paper.

TEACHING AND LEARNING METHODS

SESSION ONE

Talk about earlier painting sessions. For example, ask who in the class painted using blue to describe a happy feeling. Use the art images you have located to talk about how artists use colour to convey a mood. Share artworks by Impressionists such as Monet or Turner.

Ask children to think of warm and cool colours and write a list on the board. Encourage inventive descriptions of colours such as "freckle brown". Ask how to mix an invented colour. For example, mix blue and yellow with a bit of orange to make a "slippery green" colour. Begin Art Diary work.

SESSION TWO

Distribute white cartridge A4 folded in quarters, oil pastels and pencils. Explain that this is an experimental art session where they will practise blending colours and white to black. Begin with blue blending to red. Carefully smudge white into black. Children may use fingertips or a paper towel to blend pastels.

Experiment with each colour in the same way. Use a pencil to write invented colours adjacent to the blend. Show how layering yellow over red gives a different orange than layering red over yellow. Wipe fingertips with a dry paper towel before washing in soapy water. Complete Art Diary work.

SESSION THREE

Go outside. Children bring their own viewfinder Art Frame. Children lie on their backs and look with their Art Eyes to see the sky. Use viewfinder Art Frames to see a small piece of the sky. In inclement weather, this can be achieved through the window. Find cool colours in "angry" skies or "threatening" clouds. "Burning" sunset or "fluffy" clouds conjure warm colours. Cumulus, cirrus and nimbus can form part of their growing art vocabulary.

Share images of Impressionist artists to discuss how a painting can be like a spontaneous **impression** expressing the way we feel about landscape or people. Show prints from the school collection to show how adults use both their observations of nature and their imaginations to portray moods of nature.

Talk about **composition** and how we will use our oil pastels. Composition refers to the arranging of **art elements** such as colour and line, shapes and textures. It also refers to the way the viewer looks into a painting, how the gaze travels along the rhythms of a painting.

In this session they will complete their first oil pastel artwork on A3 cartridge paper. They will pastel an imaginary sky using only cool colours and blend using fingertips. They may choose to fill part of the sky with rain clouds. Use the whole page to oil pastel cool, wintry skies. Begin with white and slowly add colour to make a pale **hue**.

SESSION FOUR

The students are now familiar with the process of blending oil pastels and have an understanding of cool and warm colours. This oil pastel artwork uses just warm colours to create a bright sunset where the whole sky looks as if it is on fire. Encourage the use of whole page. Any child who uses the horizontal base line depiction can be invited to re-look with their Art Eyes through the viewfinder Art Frame to see and pastel just sky.

Always encourage a child who suggests an idea they wish to express which fulfills the Learning Goals but may be different from your initial idea.

ASSESSMENT AND EVALUATION

Through class discussion during teaching and through observation of the art process you will evaluate the ability of students to understand composition, warm and cool colours and oil pastel blending.

EXTENSION

Other topics for warm and cool colour use could include bushfires and rainforests.

ART DIARY:
OIL PASTELS - SKIES

RESEARCH
Use the library to find painting reproductions by Impressionist artists.

ART WORDS
Next to this list of Art Words write the definition.

BLEND _____

IMPRESSIONISM _____

_____

WRITING

Choose one painting and write about how the artist uses colour. Describe how your Art Eyes enter the painting and where your Art Eyes travel. Write the artist's name and country. Use separate paper.

LIST

GROUP ACTIVITY
Your teacher will organise the class into groups. Share the painting you chose to write about and read your description.

List all the colours you think are **warm colours**.

_____
_____
_____
_____
_____

List all the colours you think are **cool colours**.

_____
_____
_____
_____
_____

DRAWING
Draw a sunflower in warm colours.

Draw a fish in cool colours

Unit 29: DRAWING
Still Life

Teacher Guide

TIME
- 2 Sessions of 40 minutes

THEME
Still Life

OBJECTIVE
– draw from observation to develop visual perception

LEARNING GOALS
– use lines and shapes to express ideas
– represent natural objects
– represent a still life using light and shadow
– create a composition

MATERIALS AND RESOURCES

For each student:
- 6B pencil
- Newsprint A2 folded in 4
- Cartridge paper A3 folded in 2
- Art shirt

For the class:
- Still life objects

ORGANISATION

Introduce students to a drawing method where they loosely hold pencils by laying four fingers across the top. The thumb is pressing upward from under the pencil. While this hold is awkward at first, students will eventually have greater control over their drawing tool.

The A2 newsprint is folded to make spaces for four drawings. Set up three or four simple **still life** arrangements for the second part of the lesson. Vegetables, fruit, flowers or toys such as skateboards or dolls provide ideal **still life** arrangements.

TEACHING AND LEARNING METHODS

SESSION ONE

Drawing what you see is very hard work. Children will need to do some training of their Art Eyes so that their Art Hands will do as they want. Before they begin drawing, ask children to hold their pencil in the air and show how they normally hold their pencil.

Demonstrate the new way to hold their pencil and explain it will feel a little funny at first but that they will soon conquer this method and be pleased with the results.

The first drawing on newsprint will be of their non-drawing hand. The view is of the back of the hand. Keep Art Eyes on the hand not on the paper in an effort to draw exactly what we see. This is a difficult instruction to follow and anyone who glances at their drawing in an effort to "keep an eye" on their work can simply observe how some artwork is hard work. The second instruction is not to lift the pencil from the paper during the timed 30 seconds.

Some children will be looking so intently they will have forgotten to draw their correct number of fingers. Some will have drawn rather enlarged digits. The idea is to give our Art Eyes practise at drawing what we see.

Explain these are practise artworks and we can find humour as well as challenges in art. The second drawing is of the palm. Suggested timeframe is 45 seconds.

Next time children sit opposite their Art Partner and have two minutes to draw their profile. This will offer opportunity to discuss proportion. Partly because they are using pencil, many of the profile drawings will be considerably smaller than the actual head.

In the last space on the newsprint, practise cross-hatching where small lines criss-cross each other to give depth or tone to a drawing.

The Art Diary shading Drawing is completed during this session.

Session Two

For the second session, distribute the cartridge paper and still life objects. Discuss how light falls on the display. Ask students to observe the still life with their own Art Eyes. Each student will have a slightly different view. Use a 6B pencil. Fold the paper in half.

For the first drawing encourage large arm movement and fluidity of contour or outline drawings. For the second drawing discuss light and dark, where shadows lie and where the light makes the objects bright. Talk about composition and use terms such as balance and rhythm to describe work in progress so children can step back from their work to make evaluations.

ASSESSMENT AND EVALUATION

Use experimental drawings and the two still life drawings to assess developing drawing skills and understanding of composition.

ART DIARY:
DRAWING - STILL LIFE

DRAWING

Hold your 6B pencil lightly between thumb and fingers so that the nib is facing toward you. Use this space to practise shading. Begin very lightly at the top of the rectangle and move down until your pencil is making a dark line. See if you can blend so carefully that the viewer's eye cannot see distinct lines.

COLLECT

Collect two toys, one soft and one hard. Place them on a bed or chair, off the floor.

DRAWING

Sit comfortably so that the toys are at your eye level. Use your Art Eyes to look carefully at the outline and the shape of your toys.

Use a 6B drawing pencil to draw the hard toy in this space.

Draw with your 6B pencil the soft toy in this space.

WRITING

Write a sentence here explaining how you used your 6B pencil to draw different textures and different kinds of lines. How did you draw soft wispy lines? How did you draw straight hard lines?

_____

_____

_____

Unit 30: DRAWING WITH WOOL
Insects and Birds

TIME	THEME
• 2 Sessions of 30 minutes	Insects and Birds

OBJECTIVE

– explore ideas through observation

LEARNING GOALS

– research insects and draw from life

– experiment with drawing in a different medium

– develop observational drawing skills

MATERIALS AND RESOURCES

For each student:
- 1 card A4
- PVA white glue bottle for each child
- Newspaper
- Pencils 6B and 2B
- Art wipes made from material scraps or newspaper to wipe excess glue

For the class:
- Insect books
- Live insects in jars to be released at the end of drawing
- 10 balls of red, black and yellow wool
- Stuffed birds or bird books

ORGANISATION

Session One is the observational drawing of live insects, so you will need to capture sufficient insects for one between four children. If this ties in with a science project, children may capture insects. Also use a caged budgie or stuffed bird if available. Session Two has each child working at their own Artwork Station covered in newspaper with an art wipe, card, PVA glue and lengths of wool. Place extra wool in ice-cream containers so four children can easily reach to choose more wool.

TEACHING AND LEARNING METHODS

SESSION ONE

Developing observational drawing skills can be an enchanting experience for children and rewarding for you as teacher. At this level, Art Eyes are gleaning information from every possible source.

Talk about what hard and serious work drawing can be and that we can draw in many kinds of ways to communicate ideas and feelings. Here we are drawing with our Art Eyes looking from a particular angle. It may be helpful for some students to use their Art Frame to give boundaries to what they see and focus on the actual insect in front of them.

Children make a number of observational drawings of the different kinds of insects. Use a 6B pencil. Demonstrate the new art hold taught in the previous Unit and encourage use of this technique.

SESSION TWO

The glue and wool session begins with distribution of card and pencils as some students may wish to lightly sketch their design of a bird or insect using their 2B pencil. They will glue the wool. Talk about how to make bulk colour, how to coil wool, how to arrange and pattern wool to show details and show how to cut small pieces to create a texture. Also demonstrate how to lay strands of wool in waves to show a background of the imagined natural world of sea or clouds or grasses and flowers.

ASSESSMENT AND EVALUATION

This session builds on observational drawing skills, and you can evaluate ability to create using a new drawing medium. Composition and learned art ideas such as line, texture, balance and rhythm, will contribute to the final artwork, and you can comment on this development.

ART DIARY: DRAWING WITH WOOL - INSECTS AND BIRDS

RESEARCH

Scientists think there are about five million different kinds of insects in the world. Look up the word insects in the encyclopaedia.

WRITING

Write the definition of an insect here.

_____

LIST

Write a list of all the insects you know.

_____
_____
_____
_____
_____
_____

POEM

Write a haiku about a helpful insect like a bee. Remember a haiku poem is only three lines long. The first and last lines are made up of five syllables and the middle line has seven.

DRAWING

Draw an imaginary insect. How many legs will your insect have? Does it have wings?

64

Unit 31: CRAYON RESIST
Houses

Teacher Guide

TIME
- 3 Sessions of 30 minutes

THEME
Houses

OBJECTIVES
- communicate the idea of form in space
- interpret visual observations
- investigate purposes of architecture

LEARNING GOALS
- develop observational drawing skills
- create a crayon and dye artwork using drawings from memory
- compare and contrast artworks with confidence and use a growing art vocabulary
- create a crayon-resist artwork

MATERIALS AND RESOURCES

For each student:
- White, yellow and red wax crayons
- Newspaper
- Newsprint A2
- White cartridge paper, A2

For the class:
- Architectural books
- Reproductions of house paintings
- Bright yellow and green dyes in jars at teacher Artwork Station
- 1 brush 2cm in each dye jar
- Newspaper or tarpaulin
- Supply of black crayons

ORGANISATION

Session One requires distribution of red and white crayons and newsprint. Session Two has students drawing with white and yellow crayons. Invite three students at one time to complete the dyeing of their artwork. Other children can complete their Art Diary to draw one corner of the classroom or continue to add architectural details to their composition.

Build on the still life learning goals and talk about the ways we attempt to show the three-dimensional world. Distribute black crayons on request where students wish to blend to show depth or shading.

Have one area of the floor covered in newspaper or tarpaulin so that dyed work can dry. Once dye work is complete invite children to sit in a circle on the floor to discuss their understandings about the crayon and dye resist process and to compare and contrast each others artwork.

TEACHING AND LEARNING METHODS

SESSION ONE

Discuss the kinds of houses we all live in. Discuss ways in which the style and features of houses reflect their period, significance or purpose. Talk about their Art Diary research. List on the board the array of materials used in home building and the kinds of shapes and lines they discovered when looking at their own dwellings. The first session begins with an experimental artwork on newsprint using red and white crayons.

Distribute newsprint and crayon. Discuss how architects provide draft drawings when they are designing a house or school building. Each child uses their own memory drawing. Encourage full use of the A2 newsprint. This work is labelled and filed in their Art Folio.

Session Two

The second session begins with children referring to their experimental design of a house. Demonstrate how the dye rolls off the crayon on cartridge paper and explain how all the crayon work will be in white and yellow on white cartridge paper. Note that this process is called **crayon and dye resist** because the crayon resists being coated with the dye and therefore shines through the layer of dye.

Encourage the addition of architectural details and re-visit all the language they have recorded to define materials, shapes and lines. All crayon lines and shapes will stand out and contrast with the bright dyes. The more intricate and detailed the crayon work the more interesting the composition.

Session Three

The third session has groups of three children dyeing their crayon drawings. Addition of detail and completion of Art Diary assignments occur during dye work. Once this is complete take some time for Art Talk.

Encourage children's use of Art Words. Discussion of their own and each other's art will assist with growing confidence in articulating their own concepts and ideas. You can demonstrate by beginning with for example, *"I like Hana's **sharp lines** on her roof."*

ASSESSMENT AND EVALUATION

Use Art Diary, art process and reflection time to note growing confidence in line, shape, addition of detail, memory drawing and Art Talk.

ART DIARY: CRAYON RESIST - HOUSES

RESEARCH

Look carefully at your own home or apartment. What kind of shapes can you see? What kinds of materials are used in building your home?

DRAWING

Sketch from memory your own home or apartment as seen from the outside. Use your 6B pencil.

LIST

List all the shapes and lines you can see when you are looking at your own family home. Can you see rectangles? Can you see triangles?

-
-
-
-
-

List the materials in your home such as, wood, brick, roofing metal and corrugated iron.

-
-
-
-
-

While you are waiting your turn to dye your artwork use your Art Eyes to sketch one corner of your classroom. Use your 6B pencil.

Unit 32: CRAYON RESIST
Alien

Teacher Guide

TIME

- 1 Session of 40 minutes
- 1 Session of 30 minutes

THEME

Alien

OBJECTIVES

- learn a method of interpreting the illusion of space
- generate and develop visual ideas

LEARNING GOALS

- use imagination to create crayon and dye work
- invent a creature from another planet
- use foreground and background
- discover proportion and beginning perspective

MATERIALS AND RESOURCES

For each student:
- Art shirt
- Viewfinder art frame
- White cartridge paper A2
- White and yellow crayons

For the class:
- Bucket warm soapy water
- Paper towels
- Newspaper
- Violet, orange, green and blue water-based dye in jars at teacher art work station
- 1 paintbrush 2cm in each dye jar

ORGANISATION

The focus of session one is beginning perspective and creating an illusion of space. A variety of colours of crayons will be made available including white and black. All crayon work is completed at individual Artwork Stations.

For the second session, lay newspaper over the dyeing surface so that when students are ready they come to your teacher Artwork Station to use the dye. Two children dyeing their work at one time is sufficient. If there is a queue, have children name their work and set it in one pile. While they wait, their art task is to crayon the Art Diary drawings of the sun or moon.

As for the previous unit, place newspapers or tarpaulin on the floor to create a drying space for wet, dyed artworks.

TEACHING AND LEARNING METHODS

SESSION ONE

Teaching the skill of perspective at this stage of development can be compared to teaching a child how to lace their shoes. It is a real learning curve and requires innovative teaching strategies to engage the learners. X-ray portrayals and horizontal baselines are part of the art growth characteristics at this age and are innovative ways of presenting the illusion of three-dimensional space on a planar surface.

Children sit facing their Art Partner. Using their viewfinder Art Frame they frame a close-up view of the head of their Art Partner. One partner now walks to the far side of the classroom. Notice how more of the body is seen through the Art Frame.

They know they don't shrink when they walk away from their friends but they do look smaller. Individuals use Art Eyes to follow their partner carefully. How big do they look when they are far away. What has happened?

Explain how when we make an artwork we try different methods to show an object a long way away. Invite children to discuss their ideas and methods. Explain that today we are trying a method which will help us show a distant object by making it very small and placing it in the **background**. This explanation might help:

"To show a big object right under our noses we can draw it right bang in the middle of our paper. This is the foreground of our artwork. Using Art Partners is one way to learn about foreground and background. Here's another way:

On the way to school this morning Moana caught a glimpse of something in the corner of her eye. Was it a spacecraft? It moved too fast for her to know. Let's imagine an alien spacecraft has landed on the far side of our playing field. This alien craft is actually quite huge and contains huge aliens. But because it's in the distance it looks small to our Art Eyes".

Discuss the kinds of spacecraft that children imagine. Hold the cartridge paper so that you can point out a corner where a spacecraft could be drawn. It should be a large piece of paper so that you can discuss how most of the page will be left for the alien close up. Ask children to remember how big their Art Partner's face was when they were sitting very close. Imagine that the alien from the spacecraft (in the classroom!) is very close.

The crayon work is completed in an array of colours. Invite children to use white to outline their alien and black to outline their spacecraft. This will assist the viewer's eye to see the foreground straight away and then move to the background.

SESSION TWO

Children choose a dye colour and paint dye over the whole cartridge paper. As children await their turn to dye their artwork they are able to complete their drawings in their Art Diary.

ASSESSMENT AND EVALUATION

Observation of the art process and completed work offer an opportunity to comment on the stated learning goal of developing perspective. Observational experience will contribute to their enhanced use of background and foreground. Use the art making time to check in with a number of the students and note specific interactions to assist in your evaluation.

ART DIARY:
CRAYON RESIST - ALIEN

RESEARCH

Look out the window. Can you see a distant object like a tree or a building? Using your fingers, measure how big or how small the object looks to you from where you are sitting.

MEMORY DRAWINGS

In this space draw a tree which you imagine is right in front of you. How big is the trunk? Can you see the leaves?

In this space draw a tree which you imagine is far away. Use coloured markers.

WRITING

Write a short poem which uses the following words :

ALIEN
SCHOOL
DISAPPEAR

DRAWING

Imagine you were very close to the sun. Use this space and fill the whole space with your crayon drawing of the sun. Use markers in warm colours.

Now look up into a night sky and see how tiny the moon looks. Use this space to draw the moon the way we see the moon in the sky. Use the rest of the space to draw the sky. Use coloured markers in cool colours.

Unit 33: DRAWING
WITH TISSUE
Swimming

Teacher Guide

TIME
• 2 Sessions of 40 minutes

THEME
Swimming

OBJECTIVE
– explore visual rhythm in a new media

LEARNING GOALS
– draw using tissue
– experiment with line, movement and texture
– use dyes to create a composition featuring light and dark tones

MATERIALS AND RESOURCES

For each student:
• 1 card A4
• PVA glue and glue brush
• Art shirt

For the class:
• Scissors, where requested
• Pale blue, green and violet water-soluble dyes in jars at teacher art work station
• Intense red, orange and yellow water-soluble dyes in jars at teacher art work station
• 1 brush in each dye in jar
• Newspapers or tarpaulin
• Art books with images by David Hockney
• Tapes or CDs demonstrating different rhythms
• Fine tissue, 4 boxes

ORGANISATION

Each child is set up at their own Artwork Station (i.e. their usual desk transformed by newspaper over the surface). All tissue and glue work is carried out in individual Artwork Stations. Students visit the Teacher Artwork Station to paint dye onto their artworks.

Arrange the opportunity for your class to read their poems to younger students to assist with the Art Diary assignment.

TEACHING AND LEARNING METHODS

SESSION ONE

If these sessions coincide with swimming season your introduction can take place at the pool. Reproductions of swimming pool paintings by David Hockney can be used if it is not summer. How do paintings make us feel as if there is motion happening even though we know the painting is two-dimensional and is very still.

In class, have children show how they swim through the water. Ask who likes swimming.

Talk about how we perceive visual rhythms. How do we see movement? What lines indicate a flowing motion? What lines and colours make us feel calm or happy?

> *"How can we show a swimmer who is ploughing through the water at breakneck speed? How can we show a swimmer resting and enjoying the feel of the water under and around her? Let's listen to some music and think about the rhythms we hear."*

"Albatross" by Fleetwood Mac is a good example of a 'swimming' rhythm. List on the board all ideas about rhythm. Talk about dance and music in relation to visual art. Complete the first session with the rhyming poem section of the Art Diary and the Memory Drawing.

SESSION TWO

Explain how students will draw using a different technique in this session. They will be drawing without a pencil, without a crayon! They will draw a swimming pool and swimmer using only tissue then dye.

Demonstrate with student assistance ways to fold and crumple, tear and scrunch tissue paper. Next investigate how to shape torn tissue paper to create a swimming pool. Will it be a perfectly smooth surface awaiting a diver? Will the surface be rippling to show the effects of a swimmer moving through the water? Encourage repeating shapes and spaces in the water, such as, the pattern created when an arm strikes the surface transmitting waves.

Once the pool is torn and glued, the figure is also torn and glued in small segments to create separate limbs. Emphasize length, stretch, power, balance and proportion in the creation of the swimmer.

Try to avoid dependence on scissors. Only make them available if a student says they want to create an effect which can only be achieved through using scissors. Explain that we are drawing with tissue and using our hands to help loosen our Art Eyes to draw with fluency rather than absolute precision.

Each student paints with dye at the teacher Artwork Station. The pool tissue which forms the background of this artwork is dyed using a pale colour to create contrast with the moving figure where students are encouraged to use intense, bright dyes.

Complete the List assignment in the Art Diary if there is a queue waiting to dye. Lay works on newspaper or tarpaulin to dry. Display so that New Entrants class can observe the artworks.

ASSESSMENT AND EVALUATION

When all work is complete and on display, take a reflection session to discuss the learning goals. Who felt confident drawing using tissue? Who felt lost without a pencil? How did we achieve a sense of visual rhythm? Discuss how music helped or hindered the creativity.

Art Diary: Drawing with Tissue - Swimming

Research

Listen to the radio. Can you identify different kinds of rhythms such as a folk dance.

Describe

Describe the rhythm of two songs or pieces of music. Talk with your Art Partner.

Memory Drawing

Close your eyes and try to remember how your arms and legs move when you are swimming. Try to sketch from memory using your 6B pencil your swimming body.

List

Write the names of your favourite songs.

.

.

.

.

Read Aloud

Ask a small group of younger children in school if they can remember the first time they went swimming. Explain that you have written a rhyming poem about your swimming experience and that you will ask them for their comments after you have finished reading aloud.

Comment

What did your audience have to say about your poem? Did they laugh? Did they ask questions? Write down some of their comments.

Poetry

Write a rhyming poem about your first swimming experience.

Unit 34: SYMMETRICAL DRAWING
Butterflies

Teacher Guide

TIME

- 3 Sessions of 50 minutes

THEME

Butterflies

OBJECTIVE

– investigate design elements and principles

LEARNING GOALS

- explore pattern and contrast
- create a symmetrical design
- investigate insect wing patterns
- use warm or cool colours

MATERIALS AND RESOURCES

For each student:
- Newspapers
- Crayons, all colours
- Scissors
- Manila paper A2.

For the class:
- Photographic books on butterflies
- Masking tape 2 cm wide
- Stapler (1 between two children)
- Butterfly specimens

ORGANISATION

Art Diary work is to be completed prior to artmaking. Children work at their own Artwork Station with a full newspaper folded to create a soft work surface. The manila art paper is folded in half to create one set of wings using either warm or cool colours. The second session has students cut around their design and open out the folded paper to create a symmetrical design. Display can be against a wall where the centre of the butterfly is raised to create a semblance of three-dimensional form.

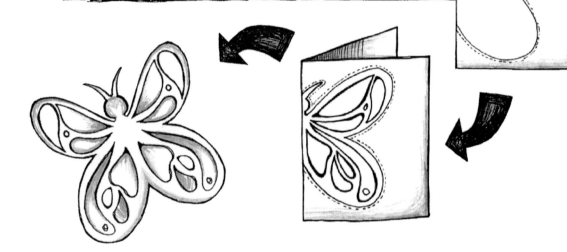

TEACHING AND LEARNING METHODS

SESSION ONE

Bring books and find web sites to show children photographs and paintings of butterflies. Talk about pattern and how identical patterns that are the same on either side of a dividing line (in this case, a dividing fold) are called **symmetrical**. At this level it will be helpful to discuss the meaning of similar and identical. Write the meanings of these and the meaning of symmetry on the board. Share butterfly specimens if available.

Brainstorm how children think butterflies get from flower to flower. Discuss their research and Art Diary projects. Provide Art Words and continue Art Diary assignments.

SESSIONS TWO AND THREE

Share sketches from Art Diary assignments. Fold paper horizontally in half to make either a tall butterfly or a broad butterfly. Discuss how Art Eyes and Art Hands will need to exercise as this is hard work. Flex and clench fingers. Stretch eyes up then down, right then left. Do this exercise at least twice during each session. Distribute oil pastels once the choice is made to use either warm or cool colours

Students complete the first half of their symmetrical butterfly designs in this session and complete the full butterfly in the third session after cutting their butterfly shape.

ASSESSMENT AND EVALUATION

Ability to create a symmetrical design and effective use of pattern in either warm or cool colours is the focus of evaluation. Take time to encourage self-evaluation so children can use their Art Words.

ART DIARY: SYMMETRICAL DRAWING - BUTTERFLIES

RESEARCH

Use library books or the Internet to research butterflies.

ART WORDS

Next to this list of Art Words write the definition.

BALANCE _____

METAMORPHOSIS _____

PATTERN _____

SYMMETRY _____

DRAWING

Use this space to sketch an imaginary butterfly. Use coloured pencils to design patterns on each of its wings. Try to make the wings on either side equally balanced, which will make your design symmetrical.

INVESTIGATION

Hunt carefully through old magazines and newspapers in class and at home. Get permission to cut out any symmetrical designs. Glue them to card and place inside your Art Folio.

GLOSSARY

abstract art	Artwork that expresses an artist's ideas or feelings through distortion of naturalistic elements
acrylic paint	A paint which uses liquid plastic as the binder. It is water soluble, but becomes permanent when dry.
adjacent	Elements which are next to each other.
appliqué	Stitching fabric to fabric.
architecture	Designing and planning of buildings, cities and bridges.
background	In an artwork it is that area which is in the distance, furthest from the viewer.
cave art	Paintings or petroglyphs on the walls of caves.
balance	Design element within an artwork which has to do with equilibrium.
blend	Fusing colours. Smudging oil pastels or wax crayons with fingertips or tissues.
caricature	Exaggeration or distortion of features with comical intent.
cartridge paper	Quality art paper. One surface is smoother than the other.
charcoal	Charred wood used as drawing tool.
collage	Artwork composed of cut or torn paper, fabric or other materials.
colour	Action of rays of light of differing wavelengths to create hues.
composition	Arrangement of art elements. Composition refers to the arranging of art elements such as color and line, shapes and textures. It also refers to the way the viewer looks into a painting, how the gaze travels along the rhythms of a painting.
contrast	Artwork showing difference such as rough and smooth or dark and light.
cool colours	Greens, blues and violets. Colours associated with cool feelings.
complementary colours	Opposite colours such as red and green, blue and orange, yellow and violet which when used adjacent to each other create sharp contrast.
contour	A line which describes the outline of a shape or form.
crayon-resist	A wax-crayon drawing then brushed or sponged with dye. Wax repels the water-based dye.
cross-hatching	Technique where pencil strokes are criss-crossed to make a fine mesh of colour and tone. Shading technique.
curvilinear	Lines or shapes made only of curves with no straight elements.

design elements and principles	Those principles and elements such as line, texture, shape, colour, form relating to an artwork.
Dreamtime	Australian Aboriginal and Torres Strait Islander beliefs of creation time when ancestral beings emerged from beneath the earth.
easel	Structure designed to support painting or drawing surface if artist is standing. Often used by landscape painters and kindergarten children.
fantasy art	Surreal or dream-like artwork.
foreground	An area in an artwork which appears to be closest to you.
geometric shapes	Mathematical shapes such as triangles, rectangles, cones, spheres, pyramids.
harmonious	Adjacent colours such as blue-green and blue-violet or red-colours orange and yellow-orange.
highlight	Part or parts of a painting which reflects the most light.
hue	Colour in spectrum.
identical	The exact same.
Impressionism	Art movement where artists painted to catch the spontaneous effect of light.
indigenous	Native or first
karakia	Prayer or incantation. (Maori)
kereru	New Zealand Wood Pigeon. (Maori)
kete	Woven flax basket. (Maori)
kowhai	The colour yellow in Maori. New Zealand tree which bears clusters of yellow flowers.
line	A point which moves across a surface. A line may be two-dimensional such as a crayon line across paper. A line may be three-dimensional such as a piece of wire.
manila paper	A brown paper.
manuka	Hardwood New Zealand shrub or small tree. (Maori)
matte	Dull. Tempera paint dries dull or matte.
mural	Large artwork on a wall often created for public spaces. In class it is collective artwork as children contribute images to create one large artwork.
negative	Space surrounding shapes or forms defined as positive.
oil pastels	Raw pigments combined with an oil binder instead of gum. They make thick buttery strokes and their colours are closer to oil paints.

outline	Line which shows the contour of a shape or form.
overlapping	Laying colour or shape over each other.
palette	A tray on which colours can be held and mixed.
pattern	A design made by repeated elements such as brush strokes.
perspective	Illusion of depth in flat artwork.
petroglyph	Drawing or carving on rock made by prehistoric people.
pigment	Powder mixed with liquid or binder to make paint, ink or crayons. Here we are making pigment from brick dust mixed with animal fat as the binder.
piwakawaka	Fantail. (Maori)
pipi	Bivalve shellfish. (Maori)
Pointillism	A nineteenth-century French painting style using small dots of colour.
polyurethane spray	Spray used to cover a surface and produce a glossy effect.
positive	Space occupied by shapes or form in an artwork .
primary colours	Red, yellow and blue. Hues from which all other colours can be made.
prism	Solid, transparent geometric form that breaks up light into the colours of the rainbow.
profile	Seen from the side, such as the human face.
proportion	Relation of one object to another in relation to size or amount, subject or degree.
radial	Lines or shapes which spread out from a common centre.
rhythm	A term used in Art, Music or Dance. A visual rhythm is created by repeating pattern or movement of lines or shapes.
rimu	Tall coniferous New Zealand forest tree.
ruru	Small nocturnal brown owl. Morepork. (Maori)
sgraffito	Technique to scrape away top layer of colour to reveal colour below.
secondary colours	Colours made by mixing two primary colours making green orange and violet.
shade	Dark value of a colour usually made by adding black.
shape	Enclosed space. Area or form with definite outline.
similar	Alike, resembling something but not the same.
space	Area around objects. Often described as positive or negative.
still life	Inanimate arrangements set-up for drawing or painting.

symmetry	Arrangement on either side of dividing line where shape and size are exactly similar, creating a balanced composition.
Tane	God of the Forests, full name Tane Mahuta. (Maori)
tempera paint	Chalky, opaque, water-soluble paint.
texture	The tactile and visual quality of a surface.
tivaevae	Methods of creating cotton quilts, such as appliqué.
three-dimensional	Having form and depth.
tint	Colour diluted with white. Pink is a tint of red.
tone	Degree of luminosity of a colour as a result of adding white or black.
two-dimensional	Flat, without depth. Artwork measured by height and width.
tuatua	Edible New Zealand shellfish.
warm colours	Oranges and yellows, those colours which make you feel warm.
weta	Various flightless, often large New Zealand insects of the cricket family. (Maori)